Poland remains one of the few
European countries in which
with the onset of the 21st
century one can still encounter
some "living" manifestations
of folk culture.
And it is to this phenomenon
that the present book is devoted.

Poland's living FOLK culture

To my Friends
from Aleksandrów
by Szydłowiec.

Anna Sieradzka
of the Staniszewski family.

HISTORICAL OUTLINE

1

page 4

IN THE RELIGIOUS SPHERE

2

page 12

ON FESTIVAL DAYS...

3

page 48

...AND DAY IN, DAY OUT

4

page 62

TO SAVE FOLK CULTURE FROM BEING FORGOTEN

5

page 84

Poland's living FOLK culture

CHRISTIAN PARMA
photography

ANNA SIERADZKA
text

Wydawnictwo PARMA® PRESS

HISTORICAL OUTLINE

The term folk culture is used to describe what has traditionally happened in the rural and/or peasant societies of a given geographical region; in terms of faith and religious observance, the habits followed both on high days and holidays and in everyday life, the output of village crafts and their workshops, clothing, music, dance, song, handed-down tales and legends. In the case of the Polish lands, a native folk culture began to develop in the first half of the 19th century as – in the different areas of pre-partition Poland there began a process of the shaping and development of separate characteristic folk genres of architecture, the output of the plastic arts and craftsmanship. Distinctions also began to emerge in regard to what was worn on the occasions of the different religious or other festivals, while recognizably local dances, songs, legends and sayings gradually started to become fixed. In art – and most especially religious art – the folk style drew on and modified models from "high art.", in particular that of the Mediaeval and Baroque periods. Examples made reference to in this way came from both the local area and from outside influences. During the times of Poland's Partitions between Austria, Prussia and Russia, a weapon in the battle to retain national identity was a conviction as to the invariability and durability of folk culture – and a simultaneous recognition of this culture as an important component of native tradition. It was at this time that folklore aroused the interest of the practitioners of high art: Romantic figures inspired mainly by folk tales and legends. Adam Mickiewicz used his ballads and dramas to take a somewhat rose-spectacled look at country people, while Juliusz Słowacki behaved likewise with his *Balladyna*. Fryderyk Chopin in turn drew upon folk melodies in his mazurkas, while Stanisław Moniuszko based his opera *Halka* around peasant heroism. In painting, in turn, all that was most picturesque and/or exotic among rural subject matter found its way into the work of Piotr Michałowski and Feliks Piwarski, among others.

In the light of the above, it can come as little surprise that the complete 123-year erasing of Polish statehood from the map of Europe led to a further intensification of folk culture's development in the second half of the 19th century. At this point, there was something of a blossoming of individually-run peasant farms, as well as a certain improvement in rural living conditions, combined with a slow rise in national and political awareness and a crystallising of rural people's aesthetic needs and tastes. This was then a good time for academics to begin to take up the study of

the phenomenon, and Poland's first ethnographer, Oskar Kolberg, proved worthy of the challenge, publishing his monumental work *Lud* ("The People") in the years 1857-1890. This addressed customs, ways of life, speech, handed-down tales and sayings, rituals, magical beliefs, games, songs, music and dances. Again, rural landscapes, celebrations, religious festivals and daily lives became a frequent topic for the painted works of the likes of Wojciech Gerson, Aleksander Kotsis or Józef Chełmoński, as well as for positivist prose and poetry, particularly that of Henryk Sienkiewicz, Bolesław Prus, Maria Konopnicka and Eliza Orzeszkowa. With a view to the development of folk crafts being stimulated and their output propagated among the urban intelligentsia, a number of exhibitions were organized in the 1880s, while the first ethnographic museums were established, and schools founded for the education of talented village youth (i.a. a timber industry school in Zakopane, schools of lacemaking in Kańczuga, Bobowa and Zakopane, and a pottery school in Kołomyja). An active participant where the last undertaking was concerned was the Society for the Support of Folk Industry active from the end of the 19th century.

As this period gave way to the early 20th century what became known in cultural circles as the "Young Poland" movement was ushered in. It was connected with strivings on the part of the cultural elite to establish a national style. A resulting increased interest in folk output was to be seen among artists and architects above all, with these finding in it a source of inspiration for the rebirth of Polish art and a bringing into sharp relief of its indigenous nature. In seeking to inspire with the building tradition of Poland's Podhale region, Stanisław Witkiewicz came up with his "Zakopiański" style, so visible in the exteriors and interiors of that area's villas and church buildings. The subject-related and formal influences of folk culture – above all those most picturesque "Old Polish" manifestations from the Podhale and Kraków traditions, as well as those of Łowicz or the Hucul area – could be seen most clearly in the artistic output of Stanisław Wyspiański, Józef Mehoffer, Włodzimierz Tetmajer, Kazimierz Sichulski and Apoloniusz Kędzierski. The propagation of folk arts and crafts among artists and recipients within the intelligentsia was an activity engaged in by the Kraków-based Polish Applied Art Society founded in 1901. This also organised exhibitions and displays. An interest in village life and customs and in the patois spoken by peasant folk also found its way into the prose of the day (the novel "The Peasants", i.e. *Chłopi*, by Władysław Stanisław Reymont, which was printed in sections in the years 1904-9 and won its author the 1924 Nobel Prize for Literature), as well as the poetry (inter alia that of Kazimierz Przerwa-Tetmajer, Lucjan Rydel and Jan Kasprowicz).

Poland regained its independence in 1918, but the country's folk culture remained a matter of no less interest to many of those active in politics, social and educational matters, economics and commerce, and above all – of course – the worlds of culture, academe and the arts. Being treated as a manifestation of Polishness, the maintenance and propagation of a vibrant folk culture was regarded as an activity that would integrate citizens of the reborn state that had long been separated from one another at the hands of the three partitioning powers. Nevertheless, the technical progress and big-city habits penetrating into rural areas after World War I did pose a threat to the continued persistence of folk culture and led to a slow but sure loss of functionality and attractiveness for both makers and customers in the country areas, let alone for the intelligentsia and the city folk, and above all for the industrial working class who simply ignored it. Deliberate efforts thus had to be made to keep the traditions in the plastic arts and crafts going, among other things through contests, exhibitions, purchases by national collections, and the setting up of regional and local musical, dance and song ensembles, as well as cooperatives and shops ensuring a demand for output. The scope of ethnographic study also broadened (i.a. through publications by Tadeusz Seweryn, Ksawery Piwocki, Roman Reinfuss and Józef Grabowski, who continued their scientific research after World War II). Professional artists wanting to maintain the native character of Polish art, and at the same time create work in line with the then trends across Europe as a whole, continued to regard folk culture as one of their main sources of inspiration, resorting above all to the forms and constructions that it had cultivated. This process bore fruit in something unique anywhere in the world in terms of its scale, namely the Polish Art Déco style manifested in all areas of artistry in the 1920s and 30s. In architecture it was to be seen inter alia in the complex of buildings forming Warsaw's Higher School of Commerce designed by Jan Koszczyc-Witkiewicz, in paintings – by Zofia Stryjeńska above all, in the graphic art of Władysław Skoczylas and his followers, in sculpture (thanks to the staff and pupils of the Zakopane Timber Industry School and especially Jan Szczepkowski), and in the furnishing of interiors, in fabrics and in other utilitarian-cum-decorative objects (above all those created by artists located at the so-called "Kraków Workshops" established in 1913, as well as Warsaw's Ład cooperative operating from 1926 on). In the international arena, the greatest renown for Polishness in

the Art Déco style was achieved as its creators took the largest number of awards at the Decorative Arts Exhibition organised in Paris in 1925.

After the Second World War, there was a diametric change in conditions that had major implications for the further persistence and development of Polish folk art. Migrations, agricultural "reform", changes in the social structure of rural areas – all brought about a further downsizing of the constituency natural to any living and authentic manifestation of folk culture. At the same time, however, the new authorities of the Polish People's Republic were for their own reasons wedded ideologically to folk culture and art as propaganda tools. There was thus no scrimping and saving when it came to money for academic study (results being published mainly in the journal *Polska Sztuka Ludowa* or "Polish Folk Art.", as well as in the form of books from such authors as Marian Pokropek and Aleksander Jackowski), for the founding of regional outdoor and indoor museums, for the training of folk artists, and for the establishment of folk song and dance ensembles (among which international fame has since been earnt by *Mazowsze*, as founded in 1948 by Tadeusz Sygietyński, and by *Śląsk*, set up in 1953 by Stanisław Hadyna). The most important role in sustaining folk artistry was that played by Cepelia (*Centrala Przemysłu Ludowego i Artystycznego*, or "Central Office for Folk and Artistic Industries" called into being in 1949. This launched a fashion for folk-related products and the organisation of associated folk events.

Notwithstanding this official thumbs-up, the decline in the demand for folk arts and crafts in Polish rural areas themselves was to combine with an ever greater influence of town culture and habits and a striving on the part of folk artists to match the expectations of a mass culture that saw their work in purely decorative or entertainment terms. The result was an ever more limited authenticity of output, which also became less and less festive and differentiated or special.

None of this changed the fact that Poland was to remain wedded to at least some "living" manifestations of folk culture. It thus became one of the few European countries to face the onset of the 21st century in such a condition that the visitor is still able to find elements of "the real thing". And it is to this phenomenon that the present book is devoted. In it we would like to present the most persistent, original and attractive examples of the continued presence of folk culture and art in Polish life, in both its festive and everyday aspects, in regard to the spiritual and the secular, and in the way that the upholding of tradition, teaching, entertainment or pure aesthetics can be served by it.

Józef Chełmoński, *Autumn*, 1897.
(The National Museum in Poznań).

Vlastimil Hofman,
*Madonna with Child and
St. John the Baptist,* 1909.
(The Raczyński Family
Fund at the National
Museum in Poznań).

Władysław
Podkowiński,
The Flooded Village,
1892.
(The Raczyński Family
Fund at the National
Museum in Poznań).

Władysław Skoczylas,
The Highland Robbers'
Dance, 1921.
(archive photo.:
The Tatra Museum
in Zakopane).

Kazimierz Sichulski,
Rafting, 1906.
(Regional Museum in Leszno).

Józef Chlebus, *Little Concert
on the Mountain Pasture,*
mid 1920s.
(Regional Museum in Leszno).

Timber Industry School in Zakopane.
Dancing Couple, 1920s.
(archive photo.:
The Tatra Museum in Zakopane).

"Zakopiański" Style

Piece of carving featuring carline thistle motif from the interior of the Church of the Holy Family in Zakopane, late 19th century.

Ornamented cupboard door from the *"Pod Jedlami"* Villa in Zakopane, designed by Stanisław Witkiewicz, modelled upon traditional woodcarving art of the Podhale region.

The wooden buildings of Podhale have a frame construction. The cracks between horizontal beams are sealed with wood wool.

The interior of the *"bioło izba"* ("white room"), festive in character, recreated in the main building of the Tatra Museum in Zakopane.

Dining room in *"Zakopiański"* style, designed by Stanisław Witkiewicz in the *"Pod Jedlami"* Villa in Zakopane.

Chapel in Jaszczurówka, a perfect instance of *"Zakopiański"* style in sacral architecture, by Stanisław Witkiewicz.

IN THE RELIGIOUS SPHERE

The most permanent, vital and original manifestations of Polish folk culture today are those surviving in religious observance and in the objects, celebrations and customs associated with it. When it arrived, Christianity did not just sweep through with its own liturgy, its rituals in the daily affirmation of faith, and its cult worship of the saintly and holy. Rather it tended also to assimilate – and to convert for its own needs – the pagan rituals that had gone before it.

The oldest linkages of religion and folk culture are to be seen in architecture and building. Catholic and Orthodox churches, belltowers, chapels, wayside shrines and crosses all attested to people's piety and devotion, being at the same time examples – even advertisements – of the artistic accomplishments of local builders, and in general a source of aesthetic inspiration for the peasant communities in which they were located. Places of worship thus often stood as absolute dominants in the rural landscape, acting as focal points and usually directing the eye vertically. The greatest numbers of buildings of this kind are to be found in the foothills regions, where the original functions are still served, in spite of the inevitable depredations that wartime destruction, the passage of time, fires or transfers to outdoor museums may have wrought. The Catholic churches erected in wood by local carpenters draw in their artistry and tradition on the stone building of Gothic, Renaissance or Baroque architecture. They are mostly single-naved, with steep roofs and soaring belltowers and covered with shingle-tiles. They have also exerted a major influence on the Orthodox building in the south-eastern Polish lands. Standing out in the latter are the Lemko Orthodox churches with their picturesque domed towers. In turn, the interiors of folk religious buildings are invariably decorated with the output of local craftsmen, painters and sculptors who transformed and "made primitive" the models they observed from "high" religious art. In this way they offered the peasant communities a direct frame of reference as regards the subject matter and form of folk painting and sculpture.

Alongside fully-fledged churches, another traditionally Polish way of demonstrating piety was the rural shrine or cross.

As exemplifications of private, everyday faith, or else serving a hagiographic or commemorative function, these assumed various regional forms and were of very varied content. Like churches, they were often placed at points in the landscape where they stood out: on elevations, on the edges of forests, beneath large trees, at crossroads or junctions, along field boundaries, by isolated houses or in the centre of villages. In this way they also served as points in the landscape at which a traveller could get his or her bearings. The tall crosses more often than not depicted a wooden-carved or cast metal likeness of the Crucified Christ. Shrines of wood or stone were in turn built to house religious carvings on their apices, under their roofs or within them, as well as – in the 20th century at least – to take sacred likenesses in the form of colourful reproductions behind glass. The subject matter of the likenesses (of wood, of stone, more rarely ceramic and, in the 20th century, mainly of plaster) includes above all the Madonna and Child or Mary Immaculate, the Crucified Christ, and especially the "Man of Sorrows", whose Late Gothic model was regarded as the one corresponding most closely with the people's faith in the sympathy God shows for the difficult lot of the peasant. The Christian cult of patron saints has also been linked in Polish folk tradition with a faith in their ability to tame the elements so often posing a threat to the lives of country people: Saint Roche extended his care over cattle, St. Nicholas kept wolves at bay, St. Ambrose took care of apiaries, St. Florian guarded against fire, while the most popular subject of all for shrines – St. John Nepomucen – still stands on islands in ponds, and by river bridges and swamps, in order to offer protection against flood.

Shrines and crosses were also erected to evoke patriotic feelings, in places where independence was fought for, and also as symbols that might repel the dark forces from the graves of suicides or plague victims. To this day it is above all in the folk religious tradition that heed is paid to the habit of making the sign of the cross in front of a church, roadside cross or shrine. In turn, the decoration of these with greenery and flowers (now most often artificial ones supplemented by multicoloured plastic ribbons flapping in the breeze) is practised not only in celebration of religious holidays (to which we will return in a moment), but also for everyday purposes. Crosses and shrines, though frequently deprived of their authentic folk sculpturework (transferred to museums or stolen to order for "lovers" of folk art) and hence adorned by substitute plaster figures and mass-produced reproductions of religious pictures (which in any case appeal more to today's rural residents), remain an inseparable and distinct element of the Polish countryside.

As has already been mentioned, the most permanent manifestations of Polish folk culture are to be found in the commemorations and customs associated with the religious holidays. Their cyclical, and at the same time biological, rhythm, corresponding with periods in the Catholic liturgical calendar, is still at least partially penetrated by what remains of old pagan beliefs, as adapted and modified by Christianity.

Standing out in the face of secular tradition is the fact that the new church year begins with Advent, the four-week period in which the birth of Christ is anticipated. In line with the traditions of Poland in general, and its folk culture in particular, Advent begins on November 30th, the day devoted to St. Andrew the Apostle. The eve of this feast day sees "Andrzejki" take place, as girls seek to read or divine meaning regarding future marriage prospects and potential candidates for husbands from either the shapes assumed as melted wax resolidifies in water, or reflections in a mirror, or the arrangements taken on by shoes thrown in the direction of a door. The Polish countryside has traditionally been less enthusiastic to celebrate St. Nicholas's Day (December 6th), yet it is in Poland above all that – from the mid 19th century on – the date became associated with the giving of small presents to children, at least in wealthier town families. Father Christmas really does come twice in Poland. The folk tradition maintains the habit of producing and buying iced gingerbread in the shape of St. Nicholas – as a bishop in a mitre with crozier. Alas these confections are now being forced out by chocolate recreations of that dwarf- or gnome-like figure in a hood and red outfit whose likeness also dominates all other manifestations of the pre-Christmas preparations.

However, an event that is really more aesthetic and artistic than commercial, which culminates in judging on December 6th in the Main Market Square (Rynek Główny) in Kraków is the competition for Cracovian Nativity Scenes. The tradition for these to be produced and presented by local craftsmen (especially seasonally out-of-work exponents of the building trade) stretches back to the beginning of the 20th century. It links up, not only with the centuries-old tradition established by St. Francis of Assisi of portrayals of the Lord's birth, but also with the Polonised, locally-set, reality of the *jasełka* nativity plays acted out by peasants who moved around the villages and towns with a mobile nativity scene. What is typical for the Cracovian Nativity Scene is the bringing together of elements of the local architectural heritage in an artistic whole made or wood, cardboard, coloured and/or shiny paper. This ensures that what were once stages for a mobile puppet theatre have become decorative works of non-professional art. They are on sale throughout the year in souvenir shops and are a source of interest to lovers of Polish folk culture, especially those from abroad.

In some Polish households, the tradition of the nativity scene is maintained through the festive season by the setting up – close to the Christmas tree – of small-scale examples with pottery, paper, wood, straw or plastic figures.

Though it is now impossible to think of Christmas without it, the Christmas tree represents a German cultural influence whose arrival in the first half of the 19th century was mainly confined to the homes of Poland's burghers and gentlefolk. The idea only caught on among villagers in the 20th century, often expelling as it did so the native decorations symbolic of plenty in the form of *podłaźniczki* (fir or spruce branches) hung up on ceilings, mini-sheaves of corn placed in the corners of a room and what are known as "worlds", put together from Christmas wafers and hung on strings from the beams. In turn, in the period after the Second World War, Christmas trees in both town and countryside were quite quickly stripped of their handmade decorations of eggshell, straw, coloured and/or shiny paper and "naturalistic" gingerbreads, apples or gold-painted nuts. Their place was taken by glass baubles, plastic stars and tinsel. Nevertheless, the diverse contemporary fashions as regards tree-trimming are as often as not ensuring a return to the decorations from folk tradition, which can be bought without difficulty in shops.

The evening of Christmas Eve (December 24th) bears witness to many persisting elements from Poland's religious and secular tradition. The white tablecloth, with a handful of hay scattered beneath it, recalls the birth of the Baby Jesus in a Bethlehem stable (though few householders now feed the hay to cattle subsequently, in order that healthy upbringing might be assured). Pride of place is still taken by the blessed Christmas wafer (*opłatek*), whose breaking and exchange between family members wishing each other well is the prelude to a meat-free meal of many dishes. While these once varied quite closely in line with the region in which they were served, they are today chosen more randomly from a long potential list of Christmas Eve fare still conditioned by religious observance (the fasting in place before the great Christian feasts) and folk beliefs (dishes made from the harvests of domestic fields, gardens and waters, symbolizing and safeguarding health and plenty). There was once a rule that there should be 12 dishes (in remembrance of the 12 apostles), and to this day there are still a plethora of fish dishes, courses including mushrooms, peas and cabbage, and cakes made with poppy seeds and honey, or fruits from Poland's own forests.

The exchanging of presents (with those for children being brought by St. Nicholas – or Gwiazdor as some regions refer to him – in greater abundance than on his own feast day of December 6th), the singing of carols (frequently of Old-Polish or folk origin) and the cosy family atmosphere, all contribute to the unique spiritual dimension and visual aspects so characteristic of a Polish Christmas Eve.

The culminating religious accent is imparted by the midnight mass held in a service to herald the birth of Christ and known as the Pasterka. In many rural churches – especially those of Podhale – this is a service that retains its strong links with folk tradition. The congregation quite often appear in regional dress, the carols may well be of regional origin and the nativity scenes presented more often than not celebrate the attainments of a given region's artistry and craftsmanship.

The Christmas, New Year and Epiphany periods were once a time for village games and spectacles full of commemorative and celebratory significance. Today there are only a few regions (mainly in the mountain foothills) where this continues.

Even then, the tradition is upheld as much to interest tourists as to meet the needs of the local communities. Carol singers progressing from home to home with a paper star and nativity scene, young people dressed up as "New Year Beggars" or "Herods", singing specific carols and recreating the polonised *jasełka* (play on the subject of Christ's birth, the flight of the Holy Family to Egypt and the punishment of Herod as he schemes to take the life of the infant), in which the dramaturgy is diversified by a humorous, up-to-the moment treatment of current affairs.

A final accent following on from the "carnival" period (which itself is treated – in village and town alike – as the best time for dances and weddings) is Poland's *Tłusty Czwartek* (Fatty Thursday), as the last Thursday in the period – occurring in addition to the more widely known "mardi-gras" phenomenon characterising the day before Ash Wednesday and known in Polish as *Ostatki* or *Zapusty*, which was taken into the peasant tradition from the culture of the gentry. Both days are designated for the heavy consumption of fatty foods (especially doughnuts), as well as for somewhat robust and noisy merrymaking, and – in the past – for amateur presentations symbolizing the transition from a time of joy to one of sadness and penitence.

The onset of the next period, the 40 days of Lent linking together a religious dimension and age-old folk tradition, is marked by Ash Wednesday. In the Catholic liturgy, this day of penitence is marked in church by the priest's marking of the congregation's heads with ash. The main dish of this period (taken on both Wednesdays and Fridays) is herring. The anticipation of the Easter festival is at the same time (in line with the natural succession of the seasons) the time of preparation for spring's arrival, the beginning of work in the fields and the cleaning of the home. Until not long ago, the spring was still welcomed symbolically by the throwing into a pond or river of a Marzanna – a dummy representing winter. Today, schoolchildren occasionally continue to uphold this old Slav habit.

A further culmination of religious/folk celebration is that occurring in Holy Week. Still celebrated in a very showy way is the Week's first day, Palm Sunday, which recalls Jesus's triumphal entry into Jerusalem. Organised to this day in

Tokarnia, Małopolska, is a more or less theatrical offering with Mediaeval roots involving the entry into the town of a wooden figure of Christ on a donkey, accompanied by a procession of worshippers with spectacular palms. The "palms" characteristic of the Polish folk tradition were and are still differentiated in relation to region – a conversion of the palm fronds scallered before Jesus in Jerusalem in line with domestic possibilities and aesthetic sensitivities bore fruit in the creation of colourful arrangements made from willow, leaves of the evergreen box, periwinkle or cowberry, and above all dry grass, cereals and flowers, diversified with blooms made from coloured paper, feathers or shavings of wood. The most-decorative palms of all – several metres long – are those from Tokarnia and Rabka in Małopolska, and from Łyse and Kadzidło in the Kurpie region, in which competitions for the longest and most beautiful specimens are held. The blessing of the palms often sees women and girls in particular outfitted in regional dress. The blessed palms were once placed in a room to decorate the frame of some holy picture – today they are usually put in a vase as a popular form of room decoration.

In only a few traditional places upholding the Cult of Calvary (like Kalwaria Zebrzydowska in Małopolska or Górka Klasztorna in Wielkopolska), do local people still put on a Good Friday Mystery Play, which realistically and expressively recreates the scenes along Christ's via dolorosa. Nevertheless, all of Poland's Catholic churches now cultivate the urban habit of an evening vigil by a representation of the Tomb with the dead Jesus surrounded by flowers and decorations, often accompanied by slogans or depictions fitted to the circumstances of the moment.

Easter Saturday brings crowds of people to church for the blessing with holy water of baskets of Easter food. In the past, this habit was elevated into a colourful folk festival. The small wicker basket lined with a snow-white cloth and decorated with greenery (branches of box, periwinkle, bilberry or cowberry), include miniature samples of Easter fare of symbolic significance: hard-boiled egg above all, but also pieces of bread and sausage, salt and pepper, and often a sugar lamb. Today, these may more often than not be augmented by completely secular symbols of life's rebirth – a fluffy yellow chick of plastic and cotton wool or a chocolate bunny wrapped in shiny foil.

In the Catholic Church, Easter Day as the Day of the Resurrection begins early with a mass known as *Rezurekcja* that incorporates a procession around each place of worship. Where folk traditions remain strongest (in the Carpathian foreland), this is accompanied by a guard that has earlier fulfilled its symbolic function at Christ's Tomb and is dressed in uniforms styled on those of the armies of yesteryear, or of Turkey, or most often of firefighters, since it is invariably from the local Volunteer Fire Brigade that those taking part are recruited. This is also an occasion for male youth to give free reign to its infatuation with pyrotechnics, with the loud reports of fireworks announcing the Lord's Resurrection shortly after dawn on the great day.

Poland's celebratory Easter Day breakfast also contains numerous elements handed on from folk culture. Foremost among these is the tradition of decorating the shells of hard-boiled eggs, in a similar symbolic gesture commemorating rebirth to that noted more or less across Europe and representing the oldest relict of commemorative folk art. Today's eggs rarely employ the old repertoire of magical or religious motifs, mainly making use of stylized floral or geometric forms. However, there are many regions of Poland in which local decorative traditions are still upheld. Batique decoration is used in the south-east, with the designs laid out using melted wax on eggs dipped in successively darker dyes (once of plant origin, but now mainly of the aniline kind). Opole-Silesia is in turn famous for its *kraszanki* – eggs that are coloured uniformly before having a dense, lacework-type pattern imparted to them with a sharp knife. In the Łowicz area, in turn, the coloured paper-cuts traditional for the local folk art are also used to adorn Easter eggs, though these are also covered with stick-on patterns, or sometimes also patterns applied using the core of bulrushes and coloured worsted, as is also characteristic for the Kurpie and Podlasie regions. It is true that the different games once associated with the decorated eggs have now disappeared, but what lives on from Polish tradition is a habit recalling the Christmas *opłatek* whereby the blessed eggs are shared among all those gathered at the Easter table, with simultaneous exchanging of good wishes. A further persistent symbol of the Resurrection is the likeness of a lamb carrying a pennant bearing the sign of the cross. The lamb is sometimes of sugar, sometimes of fired clay or plaster, sometimes of hard-baked cake and sometimes even knitted. The sumptuous Easter dishes (intended to respond to a long period of fasting over Lent) include different kinds of roast and smoked meats, hot and cold (above all hams and sausage), a range of cakes including yeast cakes baked in a savarin mould, the rich shortbread-like mazurek, often lavishly-decorated with icing and fruit, and delicacies with white cheese including cheesecake and *pascha*, whose name means "paschal dish".

Easter Monday is known as *Lany Poniedziałek* ("Drenched Monday"), since it could not possibly pass without an observance of the *śmigus-dyngus* ritual – young people's soaking of each other and sometimes everyone else with cold water. The aim here was to ensure good health and success, but it also takes on a more or less obviously symbolic male-to-female dimension. The habit, which was once confined to a more limited, courtly gesture, has reached the city as well, mostly as a somewhat grotesque exaggeration of its former self as often involving the bucket or plastic water-rifle, as it does the jug. Nevertheless, there are places in which it may also still be linked with the tradition of men disguising themselves as strange mainly female characters, notably that of Siuda-Baba in Wieliczka.

In the liturgical calendar, May is the month in which the Cult of the Blessed Virgin Mary adhered to with particular fervour by Poles is at its most visible. The afternoon services devoted to Her are not confined to churches at this time, as village women and girls recite the litany and sing special hymns at roadside and field-boundary shrines and crosses that have been particularly well-decorated for the occasion using greenery, flowers and ribbons.

The seventh Sunday after Easter brings the Pentecost-Whitsun celebrations of the dispatch of the Holy Spirit to earth. Since this generally falls in May, it has come to be identified with the colour green as *Zielone Świątki*. In the countryside, it was consequently associated with the "Maying" of homesteads via their decoration with birch branches or sweet flag leaves – also scattered over the floors to freshen and disinfect premises. To this day (even in urban areas), wreathes of sweet flag are bought to impart their particular invigorating scent to the home.

The tenth day after Whitsun, which most often falls in early June, is Corpus Christi. The festivities on this day culminate with the priest processing with the monstrance carrying the Host, before which young girls scatter flower petals, while the parishioners who have turned out in force carry flower-and-ribbon-adorned banners and *feretrony* (pictures in special frames) with likenesses of the saints. In Małopolska, the Świętokrzyskie Mountains and (above all) Łowicz, the womenfolk and girls tend to mark the occasion by dressing in regional costume that imparts a colourful, folk-related framework to the liturgical celebrations.

The eve of the feast day of St. John the Baptist, known as *Noc Świętojańska* and falling between 23rd and 24th June, was once very widely celebrated in Polish rural areas, infusing as it did a more modern Christian dimension into the long-feasted pagan start-of-summer holiday of Łady-Kupały. A faith in the protective powers of St. John was behind the taking of first bathes in rivers and ponds, the collecting of bilberries, the blessing of small wreathes (inter alia of stonecrop, thyme and asarabaca) that were hung on cottage doors to ward off fires and lightning strikes. Harking back to Slav tradition were peasants' lighting – by the banks or shores of lakes and rivers – of large bonfires through whose flames locals would leap, as well as the floating downriver of candlelit wreathes, whose movements by current and waves would offer vital clues as to the possible timing of a girl's future wedlock. Today's commercialized weekend entertainments still covered by the name *Wianki* (meaning "garlands") are largely confined to the bigger cities.

In turn, a characteristic manifestation of the age-old, still strong and vital, Cult of the Virgin Mary among Poles are August's mass pilgrimages to Częstochowa – to this day made on foot from pretty much every town in the country worthy of the name. These are timed to ensure convergence on time at the city's Jasna Góra heights topped by the Sanctuary holding the most revered likeness of the Częstochowa Black Madonna or Mother of God. The very atmosphere of the pilgrimage – of country byways being trod by columns of hymn-singing marchers, of services held in village churches, chapels and field shrines en route – is one very much in tune with country faith and the native landscape. Częstochowa is reached on August 15th, the feast day of the Assumption of the Blessed Virgin Mary, which is celebrated in Poland as the day of *Matka Boska Zielna*. The liturgy is mostly associated with the appearance of women in folk costume. Equally, recent years have brought increasing renown to the Sanctuary of Our Lady in Licheń. Pilgrimages now head there too, with masses being celebrated for thousands. But churches large or small up and down the country play host to the blessing of the *ziele* ("herbs") – in fact posies formed from whatever the country's fields, gardens, orchards, meadows and woods have yielded, as collected and arranged by the country housewife (or else in towns and cities bought in markets or in front of churches in the form of ready-made bunches).

The true harvest festival – *dożynki* – was assimilated in the folk tradition with the next religious observance in the calendar – of the Birth of the Blessed Virgin Mary. Since it coincides (on September 8th) with the next phase of work in the fields it is referred to by the term the Sowing Mother of God (*Matka Boska Siewna*). It follows the completion of work on harvesting and the first autumn sowing of winter cereals, and is therefore an opportunity to thank God for – and rejoice in – the crops won from the soil. Local squires pre World War II, and representatives of the poviat and voivodship authorities later on, were presented with harvest wreaths by their hired labourers. In turn, the owners of farmsteads took theirs to church, as they still do today. The wreaths, artistically put together from ears of corn, flowers living and artificial, were the subject of quite fierce competition even in the days of the Polish People's Republic, when the custom would be associated in large towns with performances of folk plays and appearances by local song and/or dance ensembles. These kinds of goings-on persist to this day in some localities.

The liturgical and customary celebrations of the Polish year end with remembrance of the dead, with All Saints Day falling on November 1st, and All Souls Day the day after. The Catholic reverence of saints and faith in intercession (especially in the cases of the souls suffering in Purgatory) joined together with the pagan cult of ancestors. Poland is now a country exceptional in Europe in that the graves of loved ones are visited en masse at this time, being decorated with greenery and flowers and adorned with lighted candles. The old country churchyards look particularly beautiful and nostalgia-inducing at this time, though in these too the folk-style wooden or metal crosses have for decades been giving way to tombstones, while fir wreathes and folk paper flowers are having their places taken by more permanent decorations of fake flowers.

By the second half of the 19th century, religious folk art had lost its cult character and ceased to find favour with rural customers. Most of the examples of it worthy of constituting national heritage have now found their way into museums or private collection. Furthermore, the post-War state-sponsored stimulation of creativity (led by the Cepelia chain of state-owned shops) ensured that sculpturework and painting lost the authentic raison d'etre associated with its natural environment. The interest was mainly kept up by fans of folk art among the intelligentsia, who perceived something aesthetic and decorative in folk carving and pictures, that were thus turned into "exhibits" in some kind of small-scale home museum. The same kind of reaction characterises the Podhale habit of painting on glass, also resuscitated in the days of the People's Republic and – it must be said – characterised by a strong inspirational input from local tradition and a high degree of inventiveness on the part of the contemporary artists involved with it.

Country dwellings are still presided over by "holy likenesses" in the shape of mass-produced colour reproductions, most often depicting Our Lady of Częstochowa, along with plaster or plastic statuettes again made in factories and bought in shops selling "devotionalia". Sad to say, most of these items are in the nature of kitsch appealing to the lowest common denominator and having nothing of the primitive charm that might be associated with folk handiwork.

Churches

The Church of the Mother of God of Częstochowa and St. Clement is the oldest place of worship in Zakopane, it was raised in the mid 19th century.

"Soboty" – arcades of the wooden church in Lachowice (Małopolska), late 18th century.

One-nave wooden church in Graboszyce near Wadowice, late 16th century.

Trybsz in the Spis region, 16th century wooden church with Baroque wall-paintings stemming from 1674.

Wooden Orthodox
Church in Krempna
near Rzeszów,
erected in the 16th
or17th century.

Dachnów near Lubaczów,
old wooden Orthodox
Church raised in the 18th
century on the outline
of the Latin cross.

Nowosielice by Przeworsk,
wooden Orthodox Church
from the 18th
-19th century.

The interior of the Baroque wooden church in Goźlin, Mazowsze.

Late Gothic church with a shingle roof, Popowice by Łódź.

Wooden church stylised in Baroque and Gothic character, Słupca, Wielkopolska.

Crosses

Ethnographic museum of folk architecture typical of northern Mazowsze region in Sierpc.

Sobótka at the foot of Ślęża mountain, a stone penitential cross.

Zakopane, Rówień Krupowa (Krupowa Level), Caravaca cross.

Zalipie in Małopolska region, brick shrine painted and surmounted by a cross.

Grabarka – the most renowned Orthodox sanctuary in Poland. Wooden penitential crosses brought along by the pilgrims.

Wooden cross from the rood arch of the Old Church in Zakopane.

Cross on a tree-trunk in the Ethnographic Park of Kolbuszowa, Rzeszów region.

Figure of Crucified Christ made of tree-roots, Brzegi in Podhale region.

Shrines

Roadside shrine
near Licheń.

The "Man of Sorrows"
shrine in Zakopane.

Lednogóra – a chapel
in the Ethnographic
Park of Wielkopolska.

St. Stanislas
the Bishop figure
as a shrine erected in
the Museum
of the Countryside
of Kielce Region
in Tokarnia.

Zakopane – Lipki.
A shrine with
the figure of
the Virgin Mary
in Highland dress.

St. Florian's figure
on a shrine
in Chochołów.

A shrine in the
ethnographic
museum in Sierpc.

Christmas Day

Every year just before Christmas on the Main Market Square in Kraków, a competition for hand-made "shed" with nativity scene is held.
The inspiration comes from the details of old Kraków architecture, both churches and other buildings.

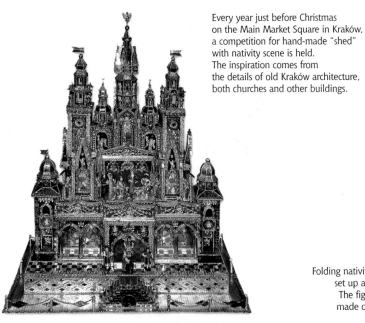

Częstochowa, Jasna Góra – nativity scene with living animals.

Folding nativity scene set up at home. The figures are made of paper.

"Carol singers" –
painting on glass
by Ewelina Pęksowa.

Contemporary
Christmas Tree.

Christmas
wreath.

The blessed Christmas wafer.

Palm Sunday

Palm Sunday celebrations in Tokarnia, Małopolska. Wooden figure of Christ on a donkey.

Tokarnia near Kraków. Members of the congregation carrying palms.

Łyse in Kurpie region. The centre of folk culture where the famous competition for the longest palm is held.

A woman from the Kurpie region wearing a traditional outfit shows a magnificent palm.

The Mystery of Our Lord's Passion

Kalwaria Zebrzydowska in Małopolska – The Sanctuary of Our Lady. For the last 400 years worshippers have gathered here to witness the Mystery Play recreating Christ's via dolorosa.

Christ carrying his Cross – one of the scenes performed in the Mystery Play in Górka Klasztorna.

Yearly recreation of the Way of the Cross in Górka Klasztorna, Wielkopolska.

Amateur-actors performing during the Mystery Play in Kalwaria Zebrzydowska.

The moment of crucifixion recreated
in Górka Klasztorna during
the Good Friday Mystery Play.

Easter

Various sorts of decorated Easter Eggs – the ones coloured in onion peel are *"kraszanki"*, the ones carrying stick-on patterns of colourful worsted or bulrushes' core, *"pisanki"*.

Traditional Easter
yeast cake.

The basket
of Easter food.

Easter
sugar lamb.

The Easter table.

Easter pastry lamb.

Gniewczyna on the Day
of the Resurrection
– guards wear uniforms
styled on those
of the Turkish army.

The *"śmigus-dyngus"* ritual
in Wieliczka is linked with
the tradition of men being
disguised as women,
known as (Siuda-Baba).

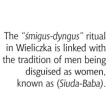

"Genuine" *śmigus* in Dobra...

...and the version on the streets of Zakopane.

The *"śmigus-dyngus"* in Dobra, near Limanowa on Easter Monday.

Easter folk ritual – *"śmigus -dyngus"* performed by the Folk Song and Dance Ensemble.

Corpus Christi

The Corpus Christi procession in Podhale is a joyous and colourful festivity.

One of the altars on the route of the Corpus Christi procession in the village of Ząb near Zakopane.

Poronin. A priest carrying the monstrance under a canopy is surrounded by celebrants in Highlandes' dress.

Fire Brigade members from Poronin are honorary participants of the festivity.

Corpus Christi celebrations in Spicimierz are accompanied by tunes performed by the local Fire Brigade Band.

Spicimierz near Uniejów. On the day of Corpus Christi the roads are covered with scattered flower petals forming fine natural carpeting.

Złaków Kościelny. Womenfolk mark the occasion by dressing in regional costume.

Watching children dressed in traditional costumes and scattering flower petals leaves an unforgettable impression. (Złaków Kościelny).

The Assumption of the Virgin Mary

Sacred likeness
of the Mother of God
of Częstochowa.

Częstochowa,
the Basilica on Jasna Góra.

Licheń, monumental buildings
of the new basilica in
the Sanctuary of Our Lady.

Warsaw, the launch day of the pilgrimage to Jasna Góra in Częstochowa. Pilgrims gathered in front of the Holy Ghost Church in Nowe Miasto St.

Zakopane – Olcza. Womenfolk wearing festive dresses carry bunches of "ziele" (herbs) to church for a blessing.

On August 15th, the day of a church fair, pilgrims from all corners of Poland arrive in Licheń dressed in traditional costumes.

Pilgrims at Jasna Góra pray lying prostrate.

Harvest Home

Vast fields of harvested cereals in Pałuki (Wielkopolska).

"Dożynki" in Żerków (Wielkopolska). Rejoicing in good crops.

Harvest wreath.

Decorated loaf of bread.

Basket of fruit.

KOZŁÓWKA
GMINA KAMIONKA

All Saints' Day and All Souls' Day

Old Cemetery in Zakopane – Pęksów Brzyzek – one of Poland's great national cemeteries, the last resting place of many of the country's outstanding citizens.

In 1984, soon after the tragic death of Father Jerzy Popiełuszko, anonymous people brought a rock of granite to Pęksów Brzyzek in Zakopane. It turned into a symbolic epitaph, by which on the All Souls Day candles are traditionally lit.

Warsaw. All Saints Day at Powązki Cemetery.

Religious Folk Art

The Pieta in Olcza parish church in Zakopane. Sculptured by Zygmunt Piekacz and Wojciech Obrochta. In the background – a typical Highland door stemming from 1887.

One of the scenes of the Way of the Cross – wooden sculpture from the Church of the Mother of Our Saviour in Zakopane.

"The Last Supper" – painting on glass by Ewelina Pęksowa.

Folk sculptures from the ethnological museum in Sieradz.

A figure of the *"Man of Sorrows"* sculpted by a folk artist.

Small wooden sculpture – a souvenir from a church fair.

Jerzy Kaczmarek
– folk sculptor from
the Sieradz area.

Ewelina Pęksowa
– renowned for her
paintings on glass.
Zakopane.

Chochołów.
The workshop of Jan Zięder
– sculptor from Podhale
specialising in figures
of saints and Christmas
nativity scenes.

ON FESTIVAL DAYS...

An element inseparable from the religious holiday past and present is the fair or fete. A day honouring the patron of a given parish will see the church surrounded by rows of stalls with "devotionalia", secular figures, cheap jewellery for women and toys for children, shooting galleries for young males and roundabouts for all. But until the 1950s or so, these were mainly a venue for the output of folk arts and crafts, as opposed to poor-quality mass-manufactured goods. What have survived to this day as a relict of the old ways are the sale at fetes of pretzels and candy floss. After the War, regional delicacies once turned out by bakeries in celebration of one feast or fast day a year only have come to be on offer permanently in some localities. Examples here include Kraków bagels (also sold for some years now in Warsaw and other cities), the decorative cockerels baked in Kazimierz Dolny and the croissant-like *rogale* with poppy seeds once baked in Poznań in celebration of the Feast of St. Martin (November 11th).

Folk traditions live on to a greater or lesser degree in the ways that great family celebrations with a religious dimension are upheld. Few old folk traditions have persisted at christenings, with the timing, the choice of godparents and the child's name, the clothes worn and the food eaten being selected at will by parents and largely subordinated to city ways. It is now in only a few regions – like Silesia – that a child's completion of its first year is still celebrated with predictions regarding future and success on the basis of the appearance of the kid and the objects it takes into its hands.

In turn, the countryside has been invaded by a citydweller's, Polish People's Republic-inspired version of First Communion, whose excesses and numerous secular touches stand in contrast with the more modest, humble, strictly spiritual celebrations once held in peasant families.

In contrast, weddings and wedding parties still retain their close links with living folk culture, especially in the Podhale region. Here both the happy couple and some of the guests don folk costume for the occasion, be this handed down through the family or commissioned specially for the big day. The dancing is

at times accompanied by a local folk band, while the actual dances join the singing and the dishes served in displaying celebratory features that are clearly regional in character.

The Polish countryside of today has also kept up certain of the traditions associated with death and burial. Communal praying and vigils around the deceased continue to take place, while funerals are attended by most neighbours and acquaintances, and wakes organized for the family.

A more professional and celebratory side of folk culture is provided by participation in events organised under the patronage of central or local government or given institutions. The best-known and most highly-thought-of examples of this kind of event include the annual summertime Festivals of Folk Bands held in Kazimierz Dolny, as well as the "Tatra Autumn" and the International Festival of Highland Folk Culture that attract many folk fans – as well as foreign participants – to Zakopane. In turn, the ambassadors for the Polish folk tradition internationally are the performers of the State Song and Dance Ensembles known as *Mazowsze* and *Śląsk*. These preserve the traditions of folk music, dance and song, if in a beautified and fully professional form. In this, they are backed up by a large number of locally-based regional ensembles.

Now visible for some time worldwide, the renaissance of interest in folk culture (especially its musical tradition) has affected Poland too, being manifested in an ever greater popularity of native melodies, as well as in the inclusion of the latter into contemporary arrangements. Folk bands and groups like Trebunie-Tutki, Golec Orkiestra and Brathanki have successfully brought out hit-making songs in which it is not hard to discern the strands of old-time folk music. This is one of the few spheres in which the folk-art tradition can genuinely be said to have experienced a revival, allowing it to persist vibrantly within contemporary mass culture.

Also associated with the folk tradition are such customs as the June antics of the *Lajkonik* in Kraków's Main Market Square (recalling the incursion of the Tartars in the mid 13th century), as well as that "must do" activity for visitors to the Pieniny Mountains – a raft ride down the Gorge of the Dunajec guided by raftsmen whose outfits are stylized versions of the regional dress in the Spis area.

Rows of colourful
rosaries sold at
a church fair in Licheń.

One of the stalls
at a fair in Tokarnia
(Małopolska).

Celebrations

Bagels.

Kraków bagels.

Decorative pastry birds.

Croissant-like *"rogale"* baked in Poznań in celebration of St. Martin's Day.

Baked cockerels – a speciality of Kazimierz Dolny.

Ginger-breads from Toruń.

Girls about to receive
Holy Communion,
in Ząb (Podhale).

The celebration of the First
Communion is always crowned
with a commemorative
photograph.

First Communion

A Highland Wedding

The bride on her way to the church.

Open church doors welcome the bride and the groom. Olcza parish church in Zakopane.

In front of the altar.

A procession of carriages with wedding guests.

During the ceremony, while all adults are in church, the little boy keeps an eye on the horses.

Young Highland girls on the way to the wedding reception.

"Bramy" (gates) are set up on the route of the wedding procession. The young couple has to pay their way (a bottle of vodka is a traditionally accepted "currency" for the occasion). People blocking the way traditionally wear various costumes.

"Pytac" – a horseman riding in front of the wedding procession and inviting to the reception – is a must at every respectable Highland wedding. Here, "pytac" drinks to the bride and the groom.

The Festival of Highland Folk Culture in Zakopane

On the first day of the Festival, a colourful procession of folk ensembles from all over the world marches along Krupówki in Zakopane.

Numerous additional forms of entertainment accompany this celebration of Highland song and dance. Folk ensembles from all corners of the world eagerly participate in the shows.

"Pytace" from Podhale ride
at the forefront of the colourful
procession comprising all
participants of the Festival.

The "Mazowsze" Ensemble

A performance
by *Mazowsze* in the *"Theatre
on the Island"* situated
in Warsaw's Łazienki Park.

Singers for Mazowsze wearing traditional folk dresses
– from the Łowicz region

... and from Silesia.

The "Śląsk" Ensemble

Festive dress from Cieszyn-Silesia.

Orchestra conducted by Stanisław Hadyna.

Once in fashion – folk costumes from the region of the Beskidy Mountains.

The *"Sieradzanie"* Folk Song and Dance Ensembles. Youth...

...and veterans.

The performance by one of the regional folk ensembles in Łyse, Kurpie.

Folk Ensembles

The "Lajkonik"

The *"Lajkonik"* on Kraków's Main Market Square appears every year within the octave of Corpus Christi. He arrives from the convent of Norbertine nuns in Zwierzyniec.

A raft ride down the Gorge of the Dunajec.

A live performance of band adds charm to the afternoon spent on the Main Market Square in Kraków.

A young raftsman wearing a stylised outfit from the Spis region.

The Niedzica Castle
and raft riding on
a glass painting
by Ewelina Pęksowa.

*Rafting
the Dunajec*

...AND DAY IN, DAY OUT

The quintessence of each geographical area's uniqueness for its inhabitants has lain in, and continues to lay in, the native landscape that arouses the interest of incomers from other landscape/cultural regions. In spite of all the changes (most especially post-War) that have affected the face of the Polish countryside, it is still possible to see many relics of what once constituted the daily scene against which peasant life was played out. There are the narrow, small-sized strips of field and meadow with boundary banks upon which the limits of some small farmer's property is marked out by field pear trees, a row of gnarled willows, or stones removed following ploughing in hilly areas. The not-too-thorough weeding of sown crops by the same kinds of farmer gives cereal crops their picturesque beauty, as the corn is joined by scarlet poppies, blue cornflowers and white chamomile. Even the mechanisation of crop gathering has not entirely consigned the sickle or scythe to history, while it is still easy to see sheaves on fields and haystacks on meadows. Some crops are still guarded against the appetites of birds, hares and wild boar by scarecrows made on a wooden frame with anthropomorphic additions like old clothes, stuffed with empty tins, bottles or even plastic bags.

Small farms also mostly keep on a horse to be hitched up to a plough, harrow, mower or potato hoe, or else to a ladderlike or board cart (albeit ones with their wheels bearing rubber tyres). Old wooden spoked wheels and whole carts often now join other generally-unused agricultural and gardening implements as a special way of decorating house facades and gardens in the countryside and also in the suburbs.

The traditional patterns of rural settlement remain – the kind typical of the Polish plains in which the buildings are largely confined along a single road, so that villages are long (sometimes exceptionally long) and thin; and the ones with "point" distributions of farms (if rarely these days in their entirely original shape), once conditioned either by relief (in the uplands and mountains), or alien influences (as in Pomerania, Mazury, Kaszuby and Silesia). A respecting of native architectural traditions as regards the type of building material

(predominantly wood) and the forms of houses and farm premises can only now be seen in a few old items of folk construction that hang on in the places they were erected. Most have fallen into ruin, been remodelled from top to bottom, or been saved by way of their transfer to outdoor museums. The regional differentiation in folk architecture has been disappearing, however, in the face of a unification of styles in the direction of the "pseudo-villa" that more often than not fails 100% to correspond with either local tradition or the landscape in which it is set. In connection with the introduction of new building materials, village houses are no longer whitewashed in the traditional way, and nor are they graced by a decorative wood-carving. In only a few regions do buildings grounded in local tradition still go up (if in somewhat modified form even then) – mainly in Podhale, Kaszuby and the Mazury region. In any case, the primary aim is now to charm tourists into staying. Standing out against this background, then, is the continued cultivation of local folk traditions in the village of Zalipie near Tarnów (albeit one that was stimulated from the top down in the days of the Polish People's Republic by way of competitions held). To this day, householders there decorate their houses, the rooms inside and all kinds of farm buildings (from wells and kennels upwards) with colourfully painted bouquets of flowers.

Also exceptional in nature are the old watermills, windmills, sawmills, barns, woodsheds and dovecotes that still survive, as well as individual small stone cellars, and even wells – not only those with their age-old "cranes" for drawing water in a bucket, but also the "more modern" ones with crank-handles.

To be met with more often – particularly in poorer localities – is the tradition of the peasant garden, surrounded by its wooden fence and filled with such characteristic plant species as lilac and jasmine, mallows, phloxes, georginias, nasturtiums and the late-autumn asters.

A further element still inseparably linked with a great many Polish villages is that age-old symbol of the country of the Vistula, the nest of the white stork. Perhaps there are now few thatched roofs on which the owner places out an old wheel from a cart or gun-carriage to attract a pair of storks to found a nest (which was always considered lucky), but these broad-winged epitomes of the countryside still seek out human habitation actively, often now choosing telegraph poles as their preferred nest sites.

In connection with the ongoing mechanisation of agriculture, the development of a trade in industrially-manufactured products, and above all the move over to a lifestyle dictated by the town, most of the traditional professions and crafts have found themselves consigned to history. Maybe sheep are still grazed in the old way on a few mountain meadows, with the flock master and his shepherds still making their whey drink *żętyca* and traditional *oscypki* goat's cheeses in their huts, but the rural landscape has lost its smithies which once not only shoed horses, but also produced and repaired agricultural and household implements to order. The place of the smiths has been taken by metal-workers, who are gifted enough in their way as they take orders for bars, railings and ironwork made to recall the styles of folk art. As peasant farmsteads no longer need pottery vessels, the few folk artists still working in ceramics have turned their attention to urban customers, for whom they make jugs, double-pots and bowls that are mainly of decorative functions. In this age of computer games and Lego blocks, children have no time for fired clay bird-whistles or wooden toys, yet the same items quite often serve a purely decorative function in the houses of collectors and lovers of folk art. Thus the items most likely to still serve their original utilitarian purpose may well be of wickerwork. Straw mats and traditional doormats still have their uses too, as do wicker baskets and other containers which can hold or carry a range of items, and are still unbeatable (being so airy) when it comes to the collecting of fruit or fungi.

Nonetheless, the inescapable fact is that most of today's folk handicrafts – which are largely confined to souvenir shops – are bought for the purposes of ornamentation and decoration. Adding decoration to what are by no means the folk costumes of fine ladies are rows of beads and amber jewellery from Pomerania and Podhale-region brooches in the shape of *parzenica*, flowery frames and patterned ribbons. Cracovian or Łowicz-region children's wear are mainly bought by Poles living abroad (above all in the United States) so that some kind of patriotic family statement might me made on special occasions. Likewise, it is mainly to the homes of city-dwelling lovers of the native folk-art that woolen or linen fabrics with folk origins find their way, serving to cover furniture, functioning as curtains or serviettes, along with table runners embroiderd in Kaszuby motifs or made from Koniaków lace. The aforementioned folk ceramics, crepe-paper flowers and more rarely straw spiders or papercuts join single items of furniture or equipment (spinning-wheels and churns) in representing particular points of interest within contemporary-style interiors. Likewise, there is no sign of any end being brought to the habit of commemorating visits to the Polish regions with the Zakopane-style walking sticks (*ciupagi*) typical of the Highlander, with dolls dressed Kraków-style, with the miniature double-pots typical of the Świętokrzyskie Mountains or with the Białystok region's earthen pot-jugs, in which the Palm Sunday "palms" of the Kurpie region can be well-displayed all year round.

Traditional ploughing methods.
(Mazowsze).

Picturesque field strips
in the Pieniny
Mountains.

Haystacks around
Gliczarów Górny,
Podhale region.

*In Field and
Farmstead*

Gnarled willows
typical of
Mazowsze.

Scarlet poppies
in Wielkopolska.

Collecting hay
in Frydman,
Spis region.

Hay is sometimes
carried in a special
sheet of cloth
(Dzianisz in Podhale).

Potato crops
in Wielkopolska.

The supply of wood
for wintertime used
to be stacked up
against the wall
of the cottage.

Traditional Rural Building

Stone farm buildings by the Biebrza river.

Whitewashed cottage from the vicinity of Sanniki, near Łowicz.

Wooden cottage from Kurpie.

Thatched cottage
in Złaków Borowy
near Łowicz.

Typical Highland
architecture presents
itself best
in Chochołów.

In Sieradz region
one can still encounter
this kind of homestead
inhabited.

Zalipie – situated north of Tarnów – is labelled "the painted village". Every year, after Corpus Christi, a contest is held there for the cottage painted in the prettiest manner.

Starościn near Kock (Lublin region). Thatched barn with a white stork's nest.

The ethnographic museum in Ciechanowiec hosting instances of rural settlements from Podlasie and Mazowsze regions.

The ethnographic museum in Sierpc – northern Mazowsze – a dovecote.

The ethnographic museum in Osiek by the Noteć river. Figural beehives.

Ciechanowiec
– ethnographic
museum of folk
wooden architecture.
Well with a crane
for drawing water.

Roofed crank-handle
well in the Museum
of Folk Culture in Osiek
by the Noteć river.

The ethnographic museum in Nowogród in Podlasie region. Watermill.

Windmills in the ethnographic museum of Lednogóra, Wielkopolska.

The garden around the cottage of Ewelina Pęksowa in Zakopane.

Lipki in Zakopane.
Grazing sheep.

Local fair in
Zakopane. *"Oscypek"*
– sheep's cheese
made to the
traditional recipe.

Old shepherd's
equipment collected
by Adam Gąsiennica
Makowski from
Murzasichle.

Polish Tatra mountain
sheep dog – the helper
of every shepherd
and the guardian
of Highland
homesteads.

Disappearing Professions

Hieronim Muszyński, a potter from the Sieradz area.

A basket-maker from the vicinity of Trzciel, Lubuskie region.

The forge and workshop of Mieczysław Biernacik in Zakopane is a home to the traditions of artistic smithing.

Decorations and Mementoes

"Ciupagi" – Highlander's sticks with axe-like handles sold on the market square in Zakopane.

Wooden salt-cellar and spoons following the patterns of traditional Highland woodcarving.

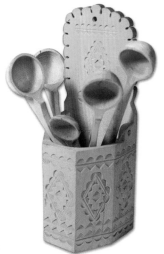

Traditional metal studs worn with Highlanders' men's shirt.

Folk culture of Podhale region finds its reflection in contemporary souvenir-production.

Dolls wearing traditional outfits from Kurpie, on a stall of a church fair.

Souvenir dolls dressed in outfits from Kraków region, sold in Cepelia (state-owned chain of stores).

Bird-shaped clay whistle from the church fair and some wooden pipes from Cepelia.

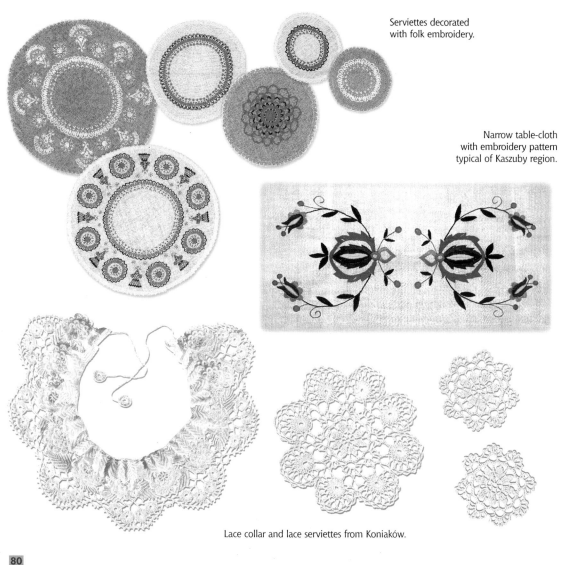

Serviettes decorated
with folk embroidery.

Narrow table-cloth
with embroidery pattern
typical of Kaszuby region.

Lace collar and lace serviettes from Koniaków.

1930s homespun
striped cloth
("*pasiak*") from
the Wieluń region.

A pillow-case
sold in Cepelia.

Pots and plates – some of the exhibits gathered in the Museum of the Chochołowskie Rising.

Glazed clay jug from Świętokrzyskie region.

Ornamented vase sold in Cepelia.

"Siwak" – a simple grey clay vase from the Białystok region.

Painted jug from Bolesławiec in Silesia.

"Dwojaki" – clay double--pots from Iłża, Radom region.

Decorative paper cut-out featuring the motif of a wedding reception in the Łowicz region.

Paper cut-outs from the Łowicz region, sold in Cepelia.

Non-glazed pottery from the region of the Świętokrzyskie Mountains.

TO SAVE FOLK CULTURE FROM BEING FORGOTTEN

If national identity is to be retained, a factor of inestimable worth is the protection, study and popularisation of the native cultural heritage from all eras and all social strata. As has been noted, where Polish folk art and culture are concerned, such activity was engaged in in the second half of the 19th century, only to be further developed in the 20th century and to continue into the third millennium. Thanks to such efforts there is a continuing broadening of the scope of knowledge on the subject of native folk culture.

The most valuable old examples of it are protected and worked on scientifically, while disappearing forms are consciously reactivated. What is indicated for those who wish to know the authentic and now-disappearing folk culture is a visit to the ethnographic museums, exhibition rooms and outdoor museums, of which Poland really had no shortage. At these places it is possible to see – if only now alas as lifeless exhibits and museum layouts – the best examples of folk art, crafts and the customs and habits engaged in on a daily basis and as holidays came and went. It is for this reason, that all lovers of Polish folk culture are encouraged, not only to observe still-extant manifestations of the phenomena in question, but also to gain a further acquaintanceship with their history.

The ethnographic museum in Sierpc.

Ornamented entrance way from a cottage in Sierpc.

Kitchen furnishings from the ethnographic Museum of the Countryside of Kielecki region in Tokarnia.

A simple interior recreated in the ethnographic museum of Tokarnia in Świętokrzyskie region.

The interior of a peasant's cottage from the ethnographic museum in Lednogóra.

Folk improvised home altar reconstructed in the ethnographic museum in Maurzyce.

An instance of wooden architecture typical of Małopolska. Ethnographic museum in Wygiełzów.

Kitchen stove from the interior of a cottage in the ethnographic museum in Lednogóra.

Exhibition of folk costumes in the Regional Chamber in Osiek.

Homestead of the Korkosz family in Czarna Góra. Mrs Maria Milonowa demonstrates how to spin wool by hand.

Home spinning workshop in the cottage of the Korkosz family in Czarna Góra, Spis region.

Private museum of folk culture established by sculptor Jan Zięder in his own home in Chochołów.

Cottage surrounded by an orchard, ethnographic museum in Markowa, Rzeszów region.

Ethnographic museum in Zubrzyca Góma, Orawa region. The manor house of the Moniaki family.

Exhibition of folk clothing in the Klamerus family cottage. Ethnographic museum in Łopuszna, Podhale region.

Interior of the chamber from the ethnographic museum in Zubrzyca Góma.

Folk Costume

Poronin. Little boys dressed in traditional Highland clothes.

Highland youth keenly wear traditional costumes on festive occasions.

"Parzenica" – the traditional embroidered design on Highlanders' felt trousers.

Fragment of embroidered design used to decorate Highland men's sleeveless jacket.

Highland felt trousers from the ethnographic collection of Jan Zięder in Chochołów.

Traditional folk clothing of the Highlanders from Babia Góra region.

A peacock feather in the cap is an inseparable part of full Kraków dress.

Traditional clothing from the Kraków region – waist-coat and *"krakuska"* – the particular sort of a four-cornered cap.

... and a little girl dressed in the "Kraków" style.

Traditional clothing from the Kraków region – bodice and white blouse.

A scene from rural life performed in the regional ethnographic museum by the girls of the *"Sieradzanie"* folk dance ensemble.

The *"Mazowsze"* Ensemble popularises ornamental delights of traditional Silesian costume.

"Czółko" – traditional women's head-wear in the Kurpie region.

"Dudziarz" from Wielkopolska. *"Dudziarz"* is a musician playing *"dudy" (bagpipes)*, an instrument typical of this region.

The youth of Sieradz region dressed in blue waistcoats.

A huge vast and colourful woman's skirt from the Łowicz region.

Children, as well as adults in the Łowicz region keenly wear traditional outfits.

Roses are one of the most--beloved motifs featured in the embroidered patterns decorating bodices in the Łowicz region.

Złaków Kościelny. The citizens of this tiny village willingly observe ancient traditions. Coming back home after the Corpus Christi procession.

Photography:
CHRISTIAN PARMA

Text:
ANNA SIERADZKA

Layout:
BOGNA PARMA

Translation:
James Richards
Anna Czajkowska (Clear Eyes Translator)

DTP:
Wydawnictwo Parma Press
(Katarzyna Woźnica)

Publisher:
Wydawnictwo Parma Press Sp. z o.o.
05-270 Marki, ul. Piłsudskiego 189 b
+ 48 22/ 781 16 48, 781 16 49, 781 12 31
e-mail: wydawnictwo@parmapress.com.pl
http:/www.parmapress.com.pl

Printing and finishing:
DRUK-INTRO S.A.

ISBN 83-7419-014-0